Relax with
Meditative Piano

40 Beautiful Pieces

Selected by
Samantha Ward

ED 23081
ISMN 979-0-001-20637-2
ISBN 978-3-7957-1572-4

www.schott-music.com

Mainz · London · Madrid · Paris · New York · Tokyo · Beijing
© 2020 Schott Music GmbH & Co. KG, Mainz · Printed in Germany

ED 23081
ISMN 979-0-001-20637-2
ISBN 978-3-7957-1572-4
© 2020 Schott Music GmbH & Co. KG, Mainz

French translation: Michaëla Rubi
German translation: Robert Schäfer
BSS 59469 · Printed in Germany

Contents

Introduction

Schott Music's *Relax With* series is designed to help you unwind with some of the piano repertoire's greatest works, alongside lesser known pieces from the Baroque period right through to the 20th century. I have very much enjoyed compiling this particular edition, including a wide range of pieces from several different genres. Many pieces by classical composers such as Bach, Chopin and Schumann feature in this edition, as well as those by more contemporary composers such as Hans-Günter Heumann, John Kember and George Nevada. It has been a real pleasure to also include a few of my own compositions as well as one by my husband Maciej too, which we hope you will enjoy learning. I have tried to incorporate as much variety within the repertoire as possible, whilst remaining within the boundaries of relaxing and meditative pieces of music. Adding one more anthology to the set of *Relax With* books has been hugely rewarding and I hope you enjoy all the collections, hopefully discovering new repertoire and composers along the way.

Samantha Ward

Samantha Ward is a British concert pianist, and founder and Artistic Director of the international festival and summer school, PIANO WEEK. For more information, please visit **www.pianoweek.com**

Introduction

La collection « Moments détente » des éditions Schott est conçue pour vous aider à vous relaxer grâce à quelques-unes des plus grandes œuvres du répertoire pour piano de la période baroque à nos jours, ainsi que d'autres moins connues. J'ai eu beaucoup de plaisir à concevoir le présent volume qui comprend un large éventail de pièces de genres différents. De nombreuses œuvres de compositeurs classiques tels que Bach, Chopin et Schumann y côtoient celles de compositeurs plus contemporains tels que Hans-Günter Heumann, John Kember ou George Nevada. Je me suis également fait une joie d'y adjoindre quelques-unes de mes compositions personnelles ainsi qu'une œuvre de mon mari Maciej. Nous espérons que vous les apprécierez. J'ai tenté de ménager autant de variété que possible dans le répertoire, tout en restant dans les limites de la musique relaxante et méditative. L'ajout de cette nouvelle anthologie à la série des « Relax with » s'est avéré extrêmement enrichissant pour moi. J'espère que vous apprécierez chacun des recueils de cette collection et qu'ils seront pour vous l'occasion de découvrir de nouveaux répertoires et de nouveaux compositeurs.

Samantha Ward

Fondatrice et directrice du festival international et des cours d'été « PIANO WEEK », Samantha Ward est une pianiste-concertiste britannique. Vous trouverez davantage d'informations sur le site **www.pianoweek.com**

Einleitung

Mit der Reihe *Relax With* von Schott Music kann man mit vielen bekannten Klavierwerken sowie weniger bekannten Stücken vom Barock bis zum 20. Jahrhundert entspannen. Die Zusammenstellung dieser speziellen Ausgabe, die sehr viele verschiedene Genres abdeckt, hat mir sehr viel Freude bereitet. Sie enthält sowohl zahlreiche Stücke klassischer Komponisten wie Bach, Chopin oder Schumann als auch moderner Komponisten wie Hans-Günter Heumann, John Kember oder George Nevada. Ferner war es mir eine Freude, auch einige meiner eigenen Kompositionen sowie ein Stück meines Ehemanns Maciej in den Band aufzunehmen. Ich habe versucht, das Repertoire so abwechslungsreich wie möglich zu gestalten, mich dabei aber auf entspannende und meditative Musik beschränkt. Die Reihe *Relax With* durch einen weiteren Band zu erweitern, war für mich sehr bereichernd. Ich wünsche Ihnen viel Spaß mit der Sammlung und hoffe, dass Sie einige neue Stücke und Komponisten darin entdecken werden.

Samantha Ward

Samantha Ward ist eine britische Konzertpianistin sowie die Gründerin und künstlerische Leiterin von PIANO WEEK, einem internationalen Festival und Ferienkurs. Weitere Informationen finden Sie unter **www.pianoweek.com**

When Paris Dreams

George Nevada
1939–2014

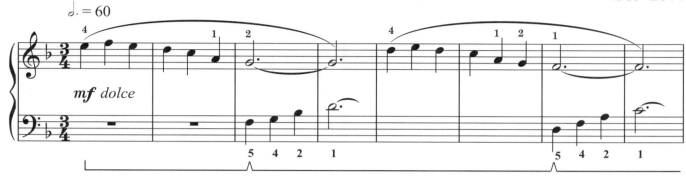

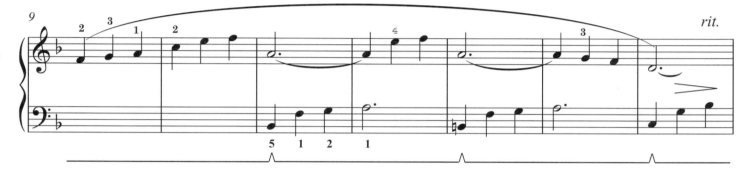

From the Schott edition *Romantic Miniatures* (ED 7696)

Like a Feather in the Wind

Hans-Günter Heumann
*1955

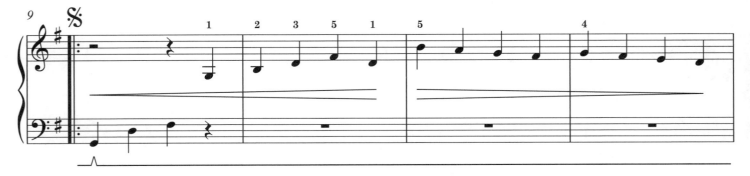

From the Schott edition *Live Your Dream* (ED 21100)

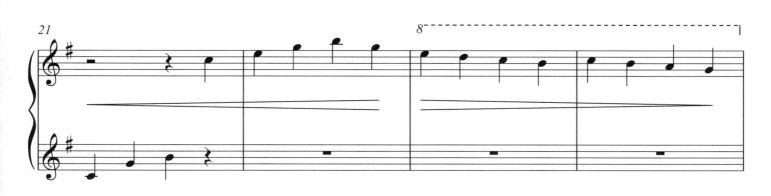

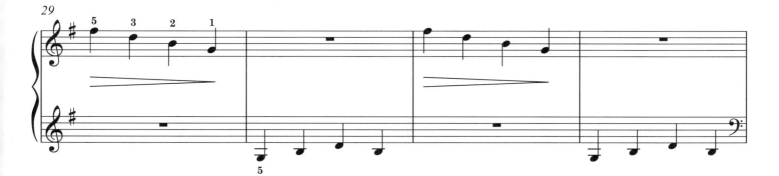

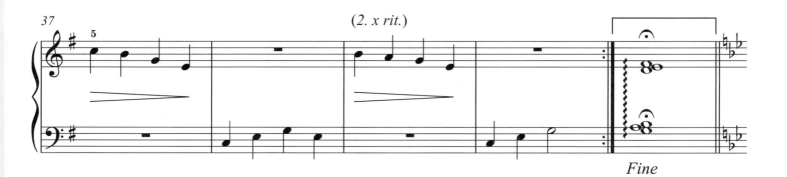

Fine

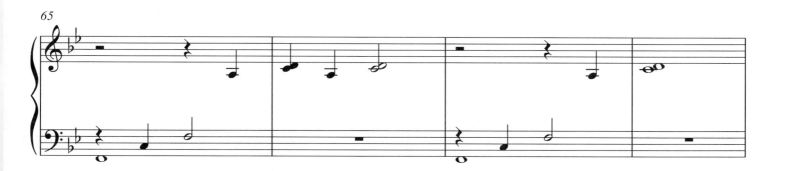

rit.

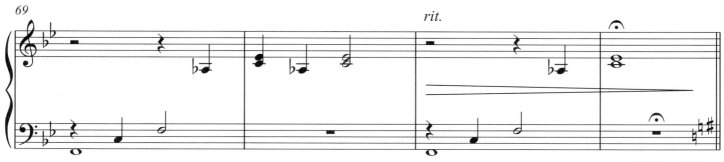

D.S. al Fine

Lullaby
from *Trinkets*, Op. 93/4

Paul Zilcher
1855–1943

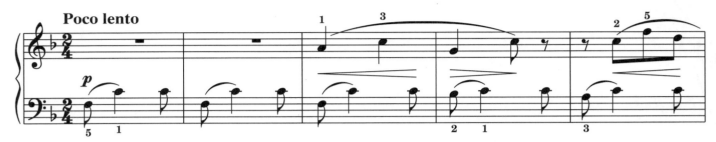

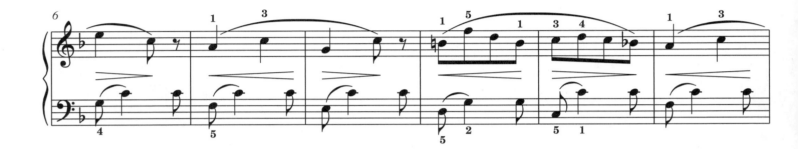

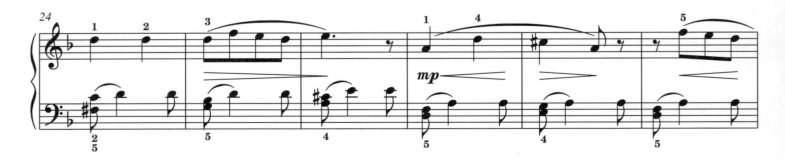

From the Schott edition *Night and Dreams* (ED 9048)

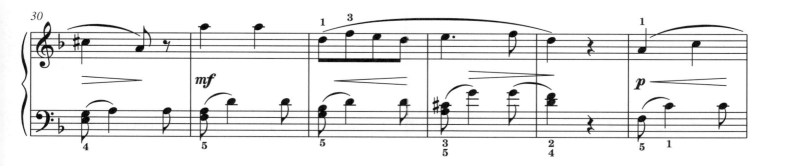

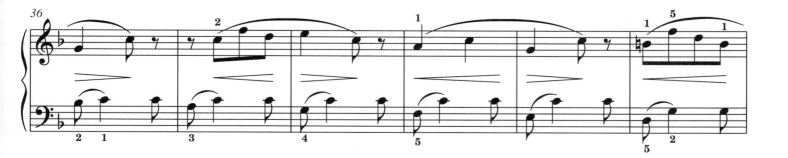

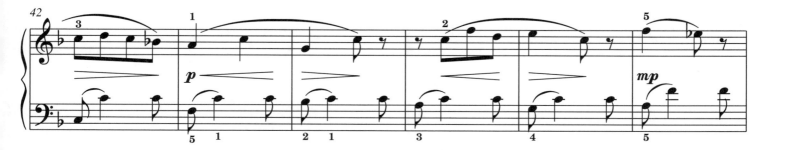

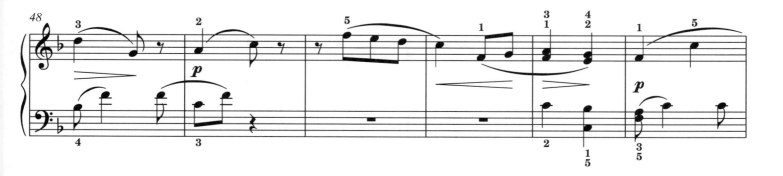

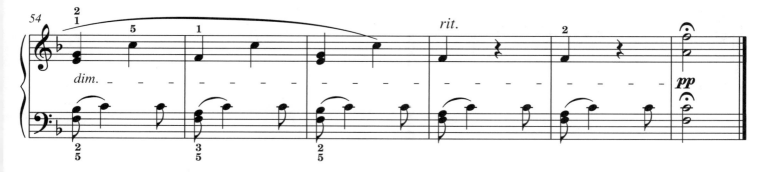

Sad Song

Jürgen Moser
*1949

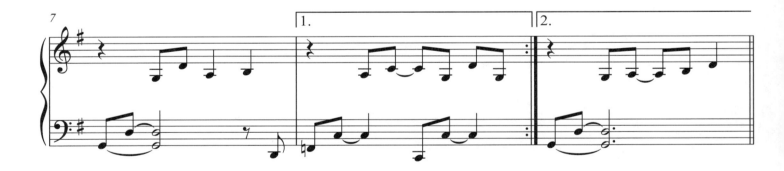

From the Schott edition *Beginning Rock Piano* (ED 9503)

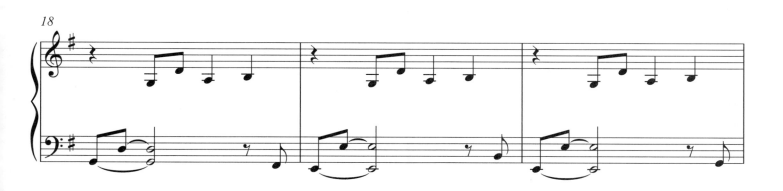

Song of the Fisherwomen

Georges Ivanovich Gurdjieff
1866–1949
Thomas de Hartmann
1885–1956

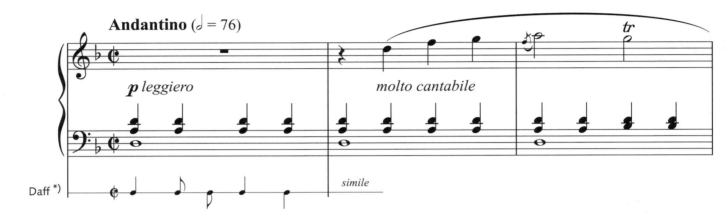

From the Schott edition *Music for the Piano* (ED 7841)
*) Daff: Persian and Arabian frame drum.

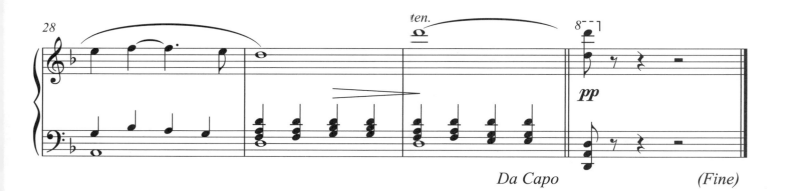

Da Capo   *(Fine)*

Evening Flower
Abendblume

Barbara Heller
*1936

Free tempo and phrasing (quasi improvisando)

From the Schott edition *Musical Flowers* (ED 20374)

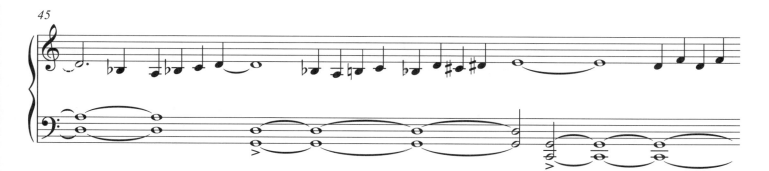

improvise ad libitum

Inflections

Melanie Spanswick
*1969

Tranquillo (♩ = 96-104)

From the Schott edition *No Words Necessary* (ED 23075)

Soft Blue

John Kember
*1935

From the Schott edition *On the Lighter Side* (ED 12726)

For Emily Pearl Campbell

Tango for Em

Samantha Ward
*1982

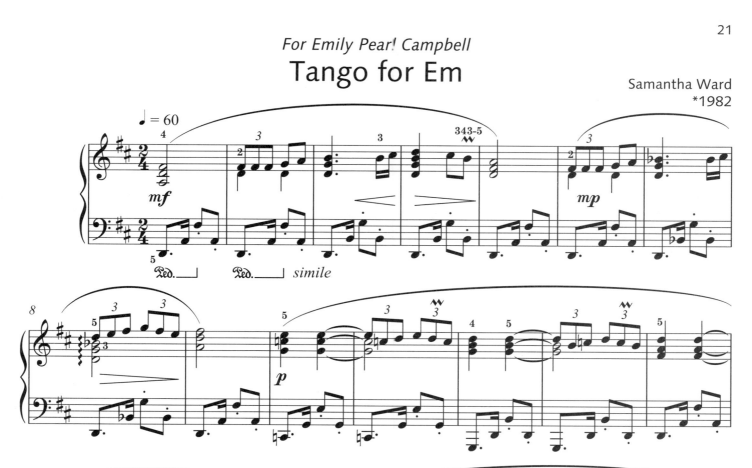

Melancholy Reflections

Mike Schoenmehl
*1957

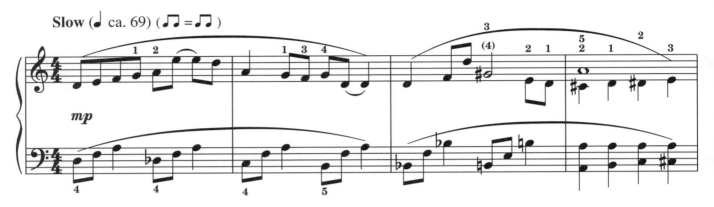

From the Schott edition *Piano Studies in Pop* (ED 7304)

Lost in Thought

Melanie Spanswick
*1969

From the Schott edition *No Words Necessary* (ED 23075)

für Peter Hanser-Strecker zum 70. Geburtstag

Two Steps Forward, One Step Back

Zwei Schritte vor, ein Schritt zurück

Peter Michael Hamel
*1947

From the Schott edition *Dances of Our Time* (ED 21470)
*) two-step crab dance

Walking in the Wood

Melanie Spanswick
*1969

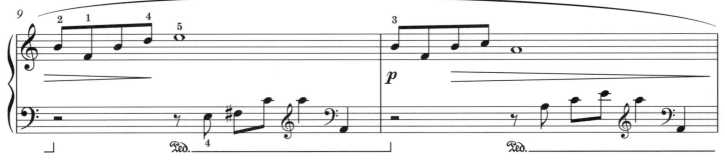

From the Schott edition *No Words Necessary* (ED 23075)

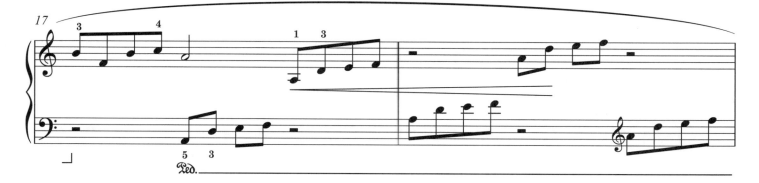

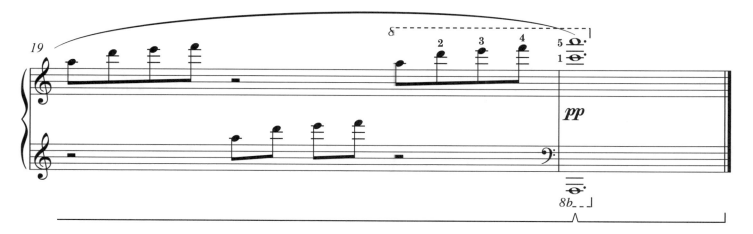

Little Atlantic Rhapsody

George Nevada
1939–2014

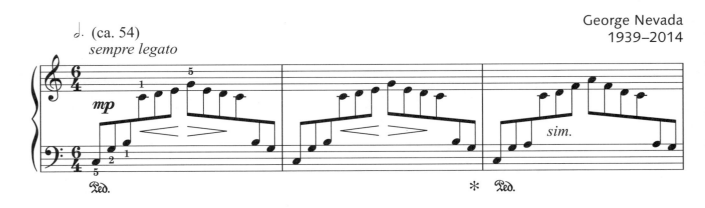

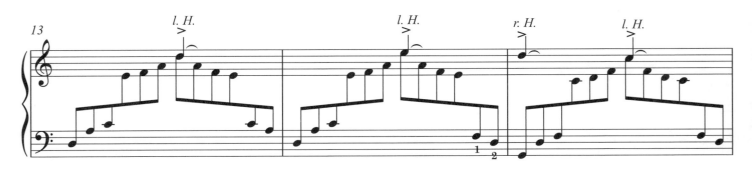

From the Schott edition *Romantic Miniatures* (ED 7696)

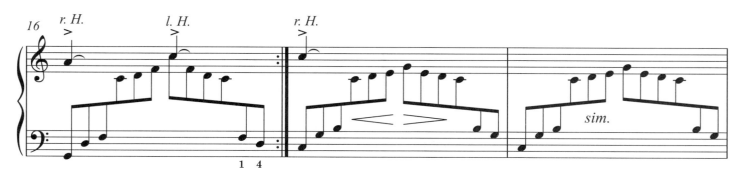

D. S. con rep.

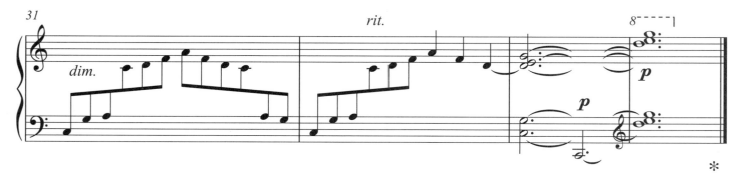

For my husband Maciej

Slow Blues

Samantha Ward
*1982

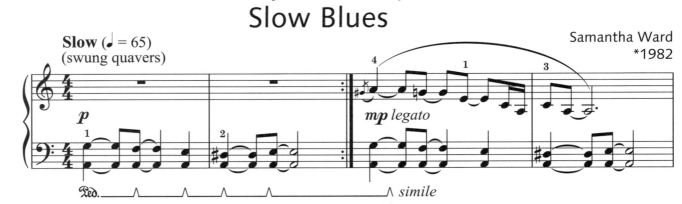

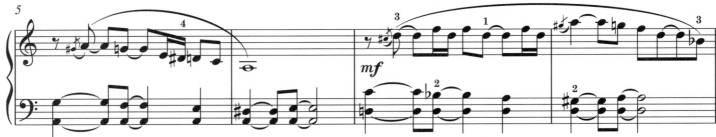

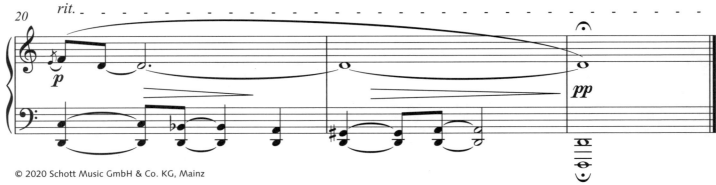

Lullaby

Johanna Senfter
1879–1961

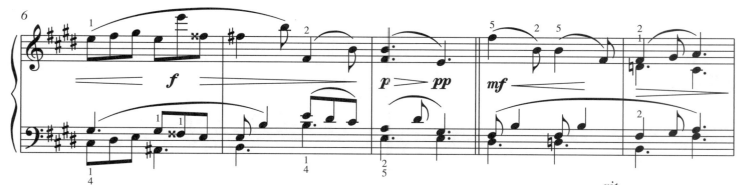

From the Schott edition *6 Easy Pieces for Beginners* (ED0 9773)
Fingerings are by Johanna Senfter

Sentimental Lady

Eduard Pütz
1911–2000

From the Schott edition *Waltzing the Blues* (ED 8033)

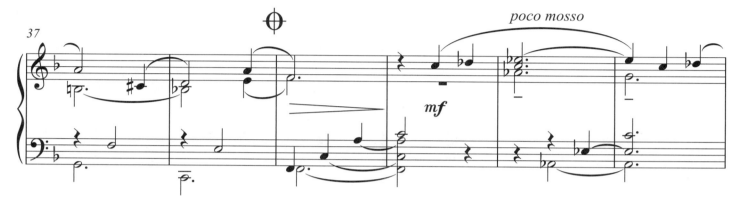

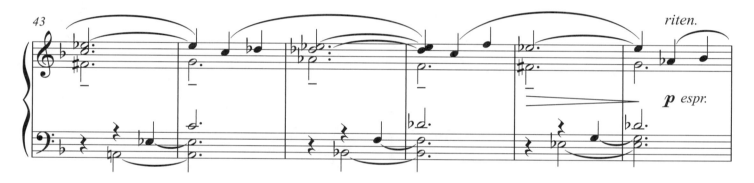

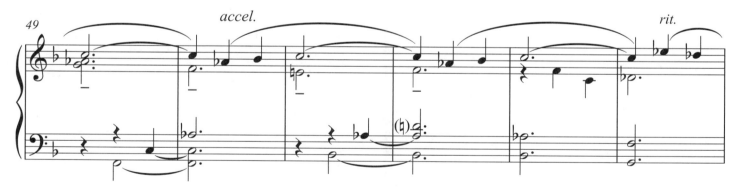

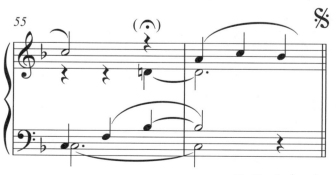

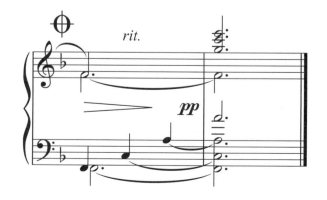

D. S. al ⊕-⊕

Prelude
B minor

Johann Sebastian Bach
1685–1750
Arr.: Alexander Siloti

after: J.S. Bach, Prelude E minor, BWV 855a (from: Klavierbüchlein für Wilhelm Friedemann Bach)
From the Schott edition *Concert Favourites* (ED 21827)
*) Arpeggio only in the repetition; bring out minims and semibreves in the repetition (note of the editor)

Notturno No. 2
[1st version]
S 541a [192a]

Franz Liszt
1811–1886

Lento espressivo

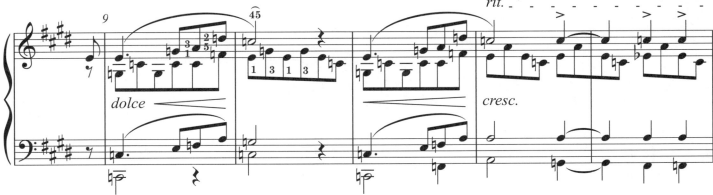

From the Schott edition *Album Leaves and Short Piano Pieces* (ED 9054)

Midnight Blue

John Kember
*1935

Dreamily ♩ = 80
Straight Quavers

From the Schott edition *On the Lighter Side* (ED 12614)

Child Falling Asleep

from *Scenes from Childhood*, Op. 15/12

Robert Schumann
1810–1856

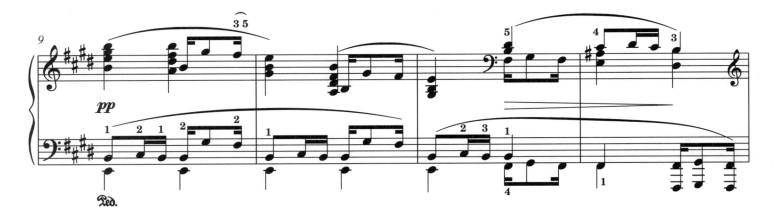

From the Schott edition *Programme Music* (ED 9043)

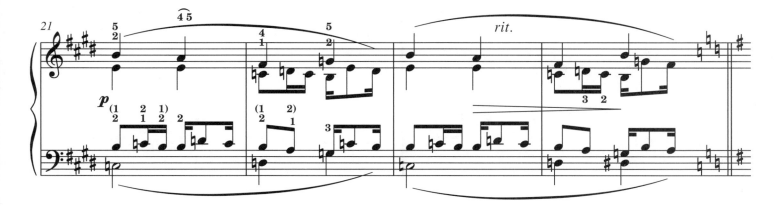

Meditation
from *Music Diary*

The colorful clouds sail in the sky;
how I wish they could take me to travel !

Zhang Zhao
*1964

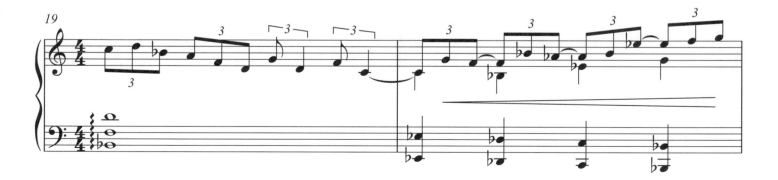

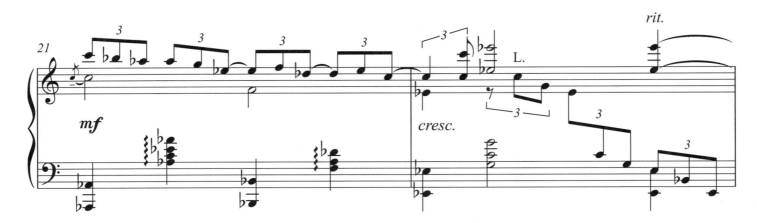

Lento (♩ = 60)

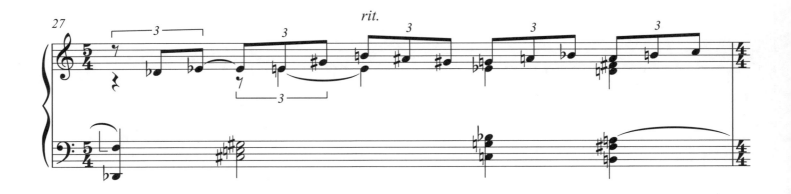

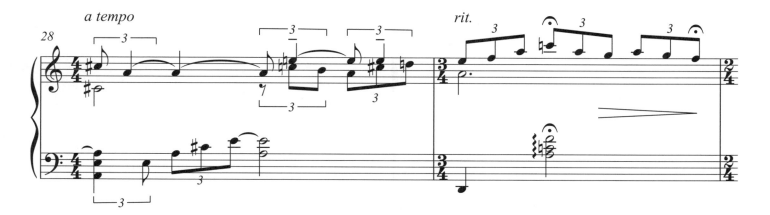

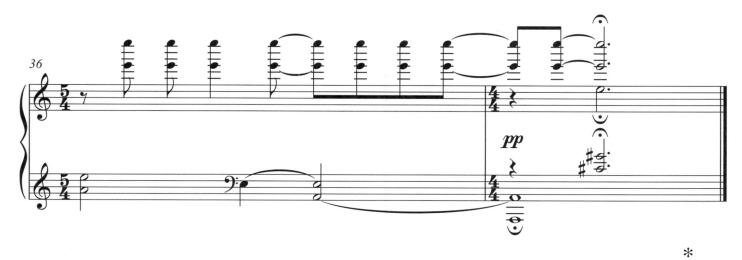

*

Listen to Your Heart

Hans-Günter Heumann
*1955

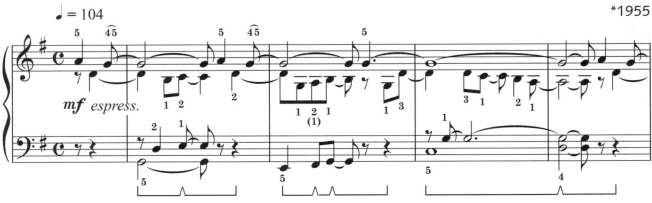

From the Schott edition *Go Your Own Way* (ED 22262)

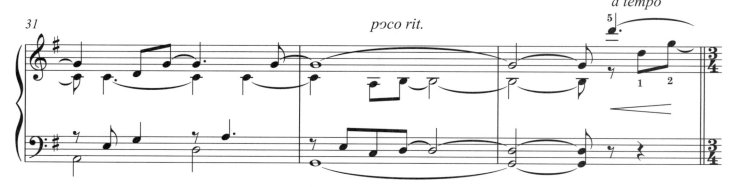

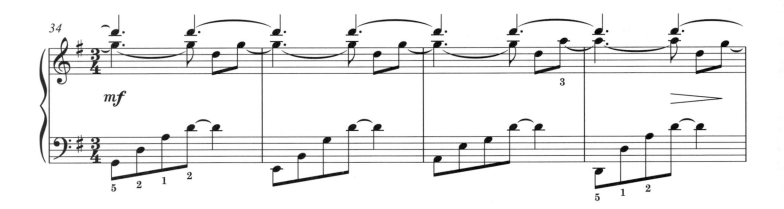

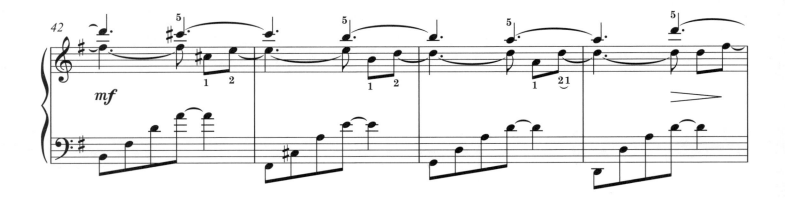

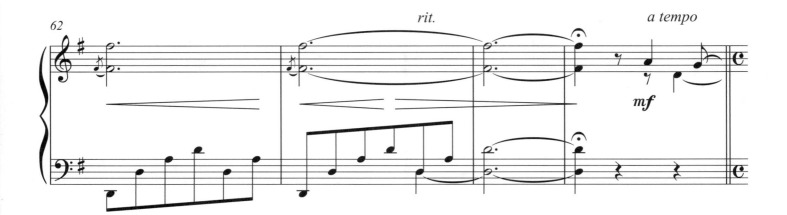

Lamentation
from *Pastelle*, Op. 3/1

Alexander Gretchaninoff
1864–1956

Andantino

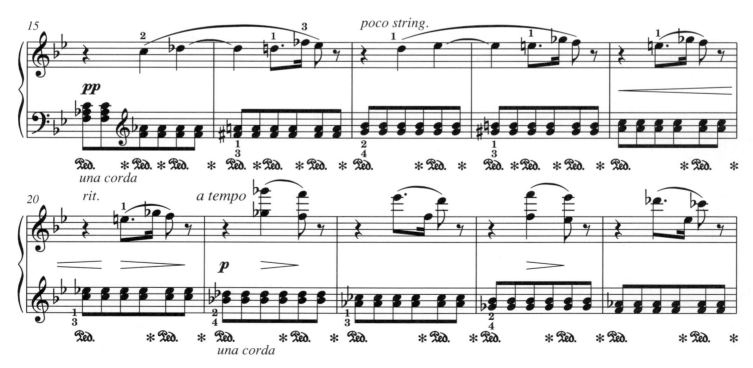

From the Schott edition *Emotions* (ED 9045)

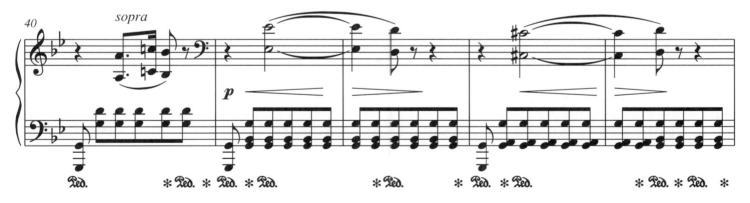

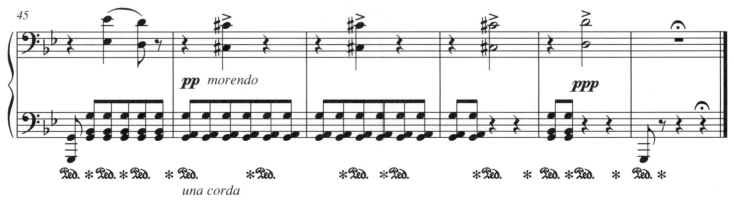

Elegy
from *Lyric Pieces*, Op. 38/6

Edvard Grieg
1843–1907

Allegretto semplice

From the Schott edition *Emotions* (ED 9045)

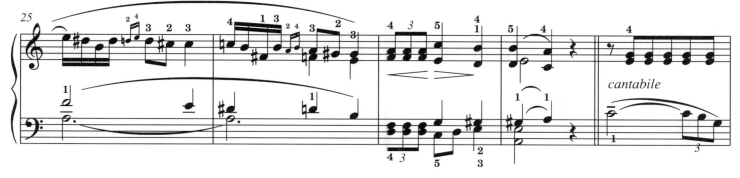

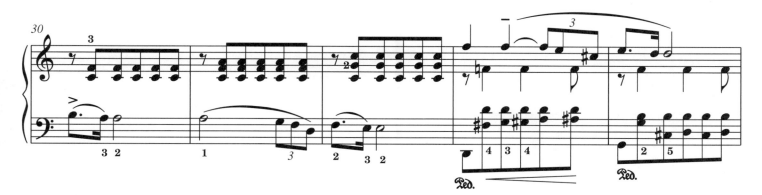

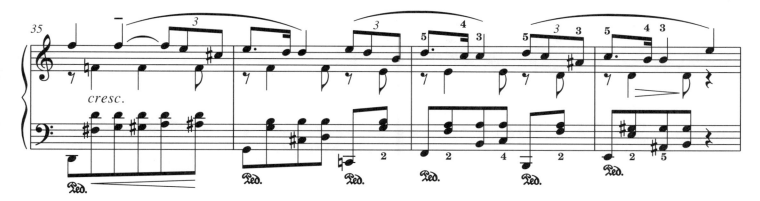

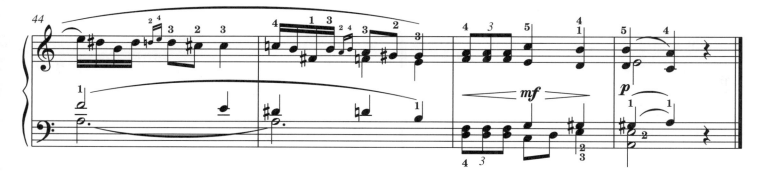

Lullaby

Robert Fuchs
1847–1927

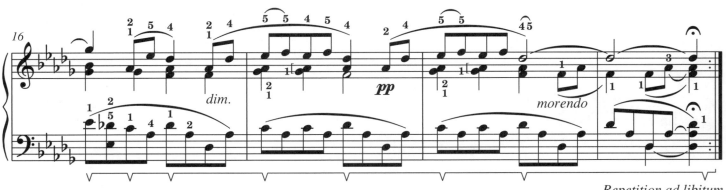

Repetition ad libitum

From the Schott edition *Night and Dreams* (ED 9048)

Prélude
Op. 27/2

Alexander Scriabin
1871–1915

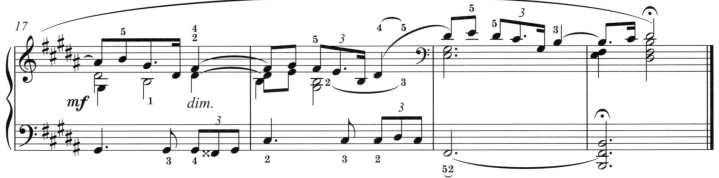

Prélude
from *España*, Op. 165/1

Isaac Albéniz
1860–1909

Andantino

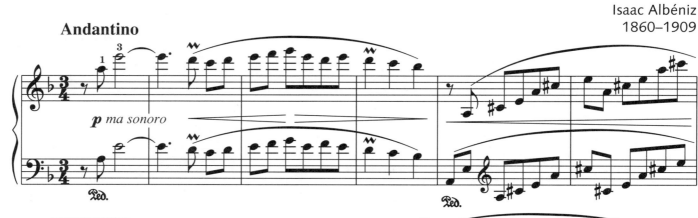

From the Schott edition *Impressionism* (ED 9042)

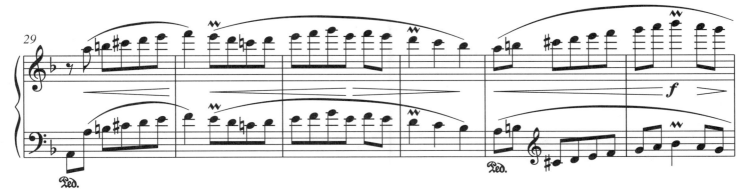

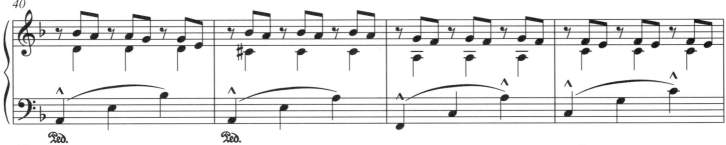

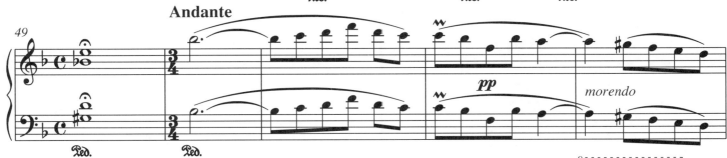

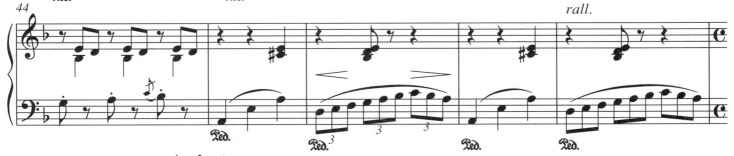

Margarita, Daughter of May

from *Enchanted City*

Mikis Theodorakis
*1925
Arr.: Tatiana Papageorgiou

From the Schott edition *Songs for Piano* (ED 21060)

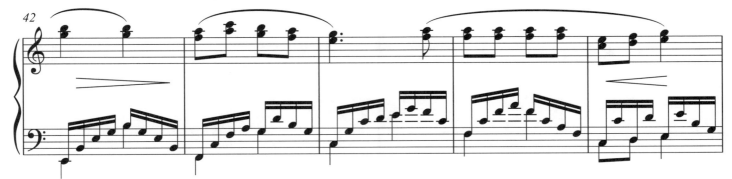

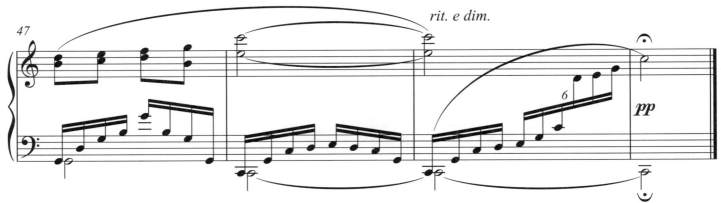

Dedicated to Peter James Corney

Impressions on E.D.

I LOST a world the other day.
Has anybody found?
You'll know it by the row of stars
Around its forehead bound.

A rich man might not notice it;
Yet to my frugal eye
Of more esteem than ducats.
Oh, find it, sir, for me!

Emily Dickinson (1830–86)

Maciej Raginia
*1983

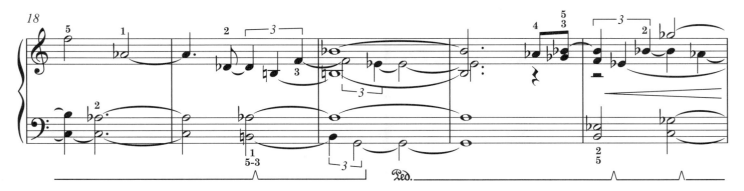

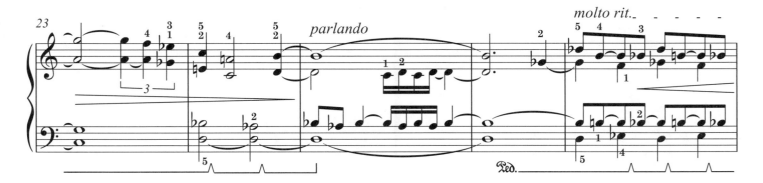

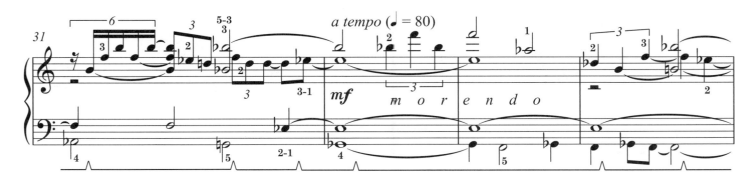

Ave Maria
Méditation sur le Premier Prélude de J. S. Bach

Charles Gounod
1818–1893

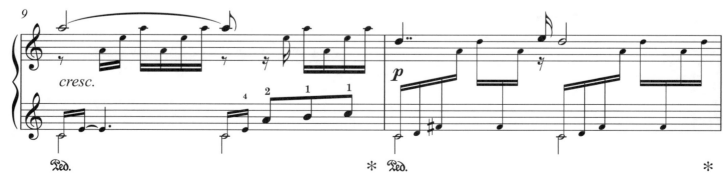

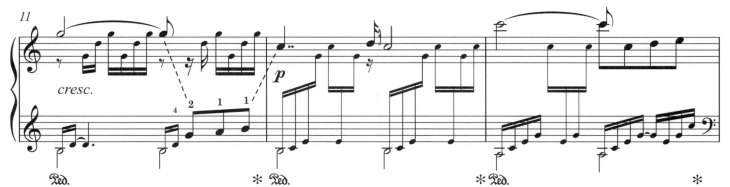

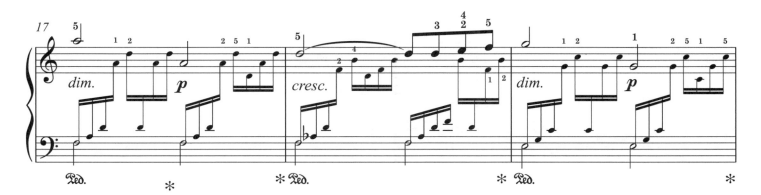

Barcarolle
Op. 65/6

Charles-Valentin Alkan
1813–1888

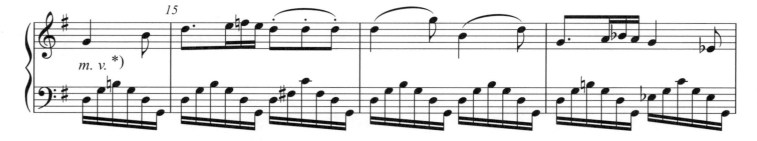

*) m. v. = mezzo voce (*mf*)

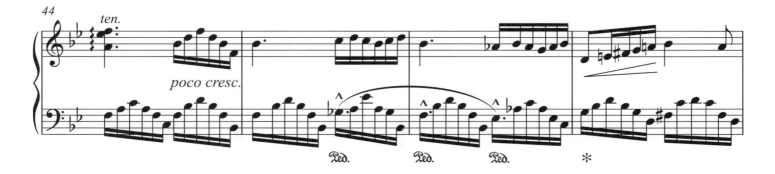

Méditation
from *Thaïs*

Jules Massenet
1842–1912
Arr.: Hans-Günter Heumann

Andante religioso (♩ = 60)

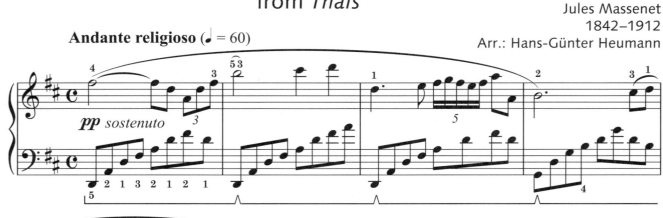

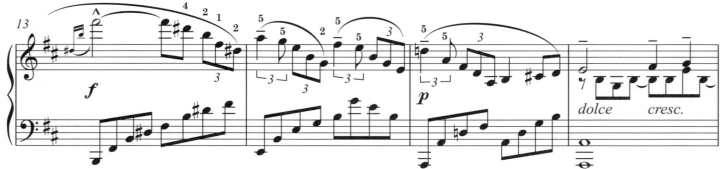

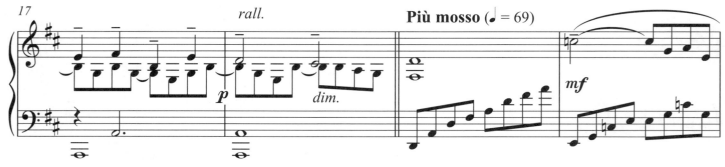

From the Schott edition *La Donna è mobile* (ED 21129)

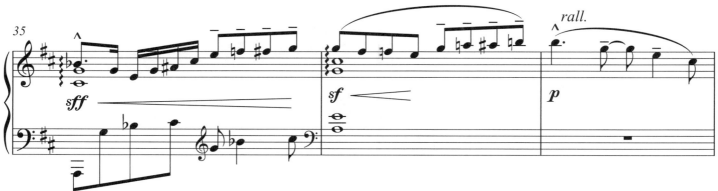

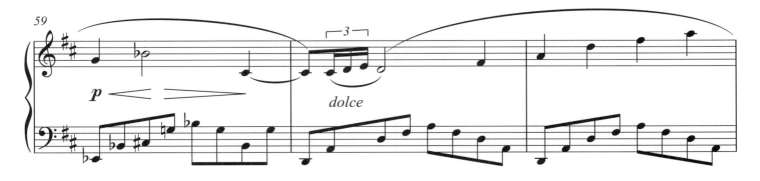

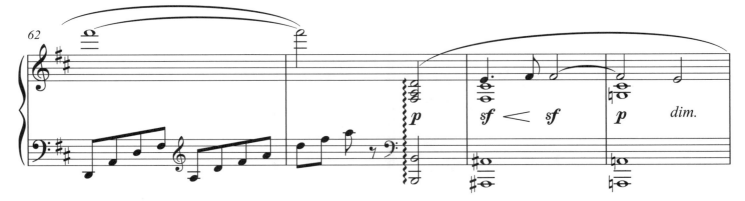

Air in Blue
based on the Orchestral Suite No. 3 by J. S. Bach

Uwe Korn
*1962

From the Schott edition *Classics Meat Jazz 2* (ED 20537)

Sheherazade
from *Album for the Young*, Op. 68/32

Robert Schumann
1810–1856

Ziemlich langsam, leise

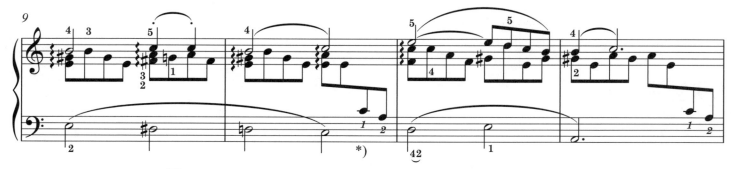

From the Schott edition *Portraits* (ED 22632)
*) fingering in italics by Schumann

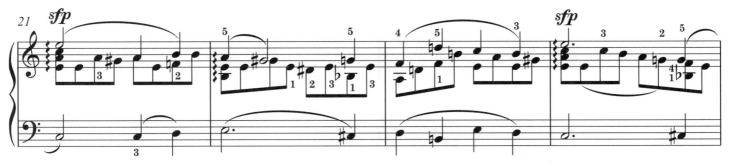

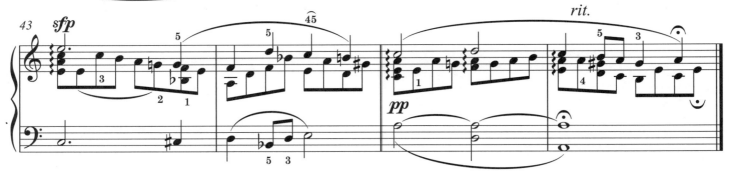

Sentimental Melody

Aaron Copland
1900–1990

Non allegro, legato

From the Schott edition *Emotions* (ED 9045)

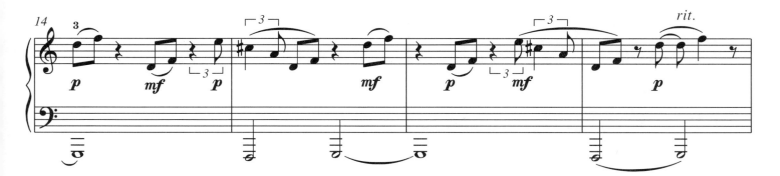

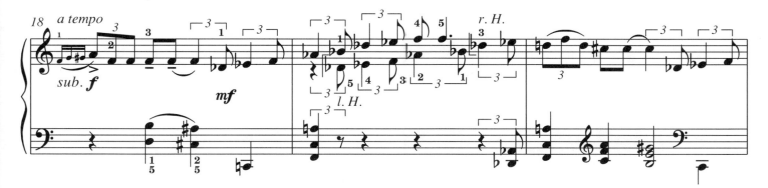

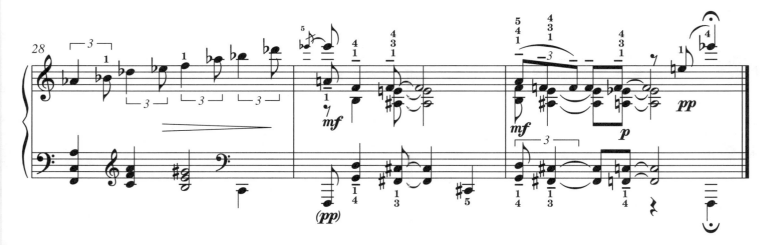

Notturno
from *Lyric Pieces*, Op. 54/4

Edvard Grieg
1843–1907

Andante

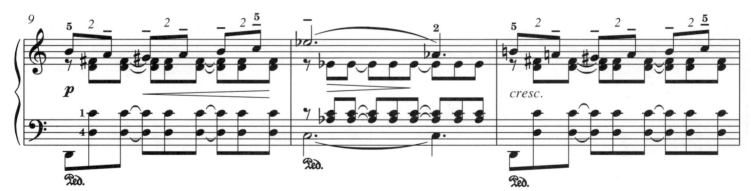

From the Schott edition *Night and Dreams* (ED 9048)

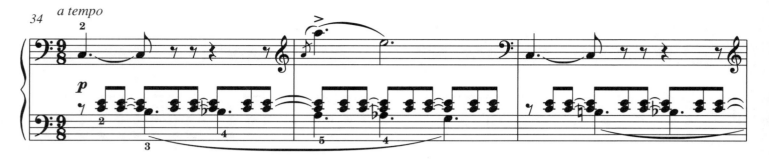

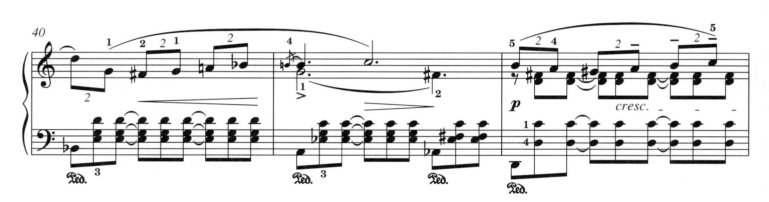

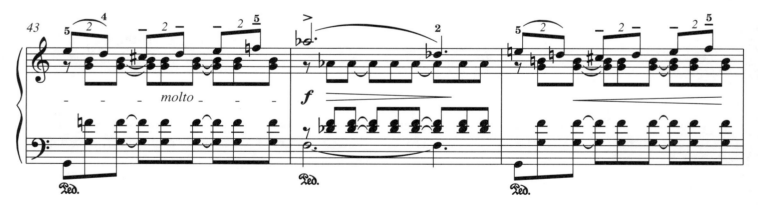

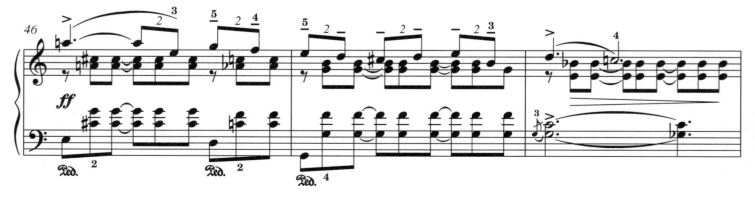

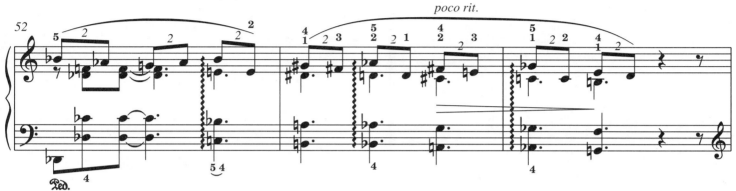

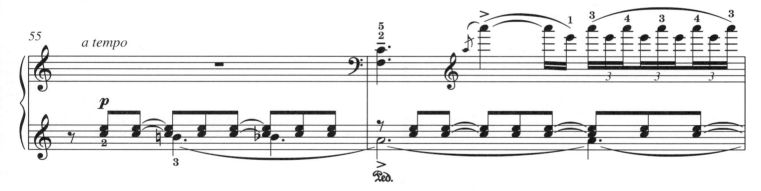

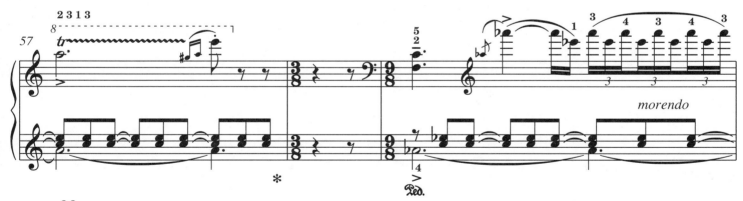

Prélude
Op. 28/13

Frédéric Chopin
1810–1849

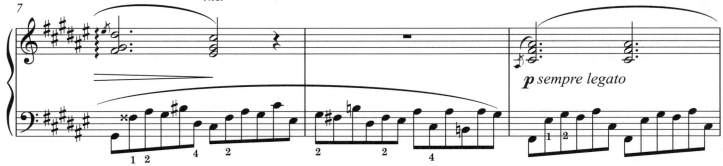

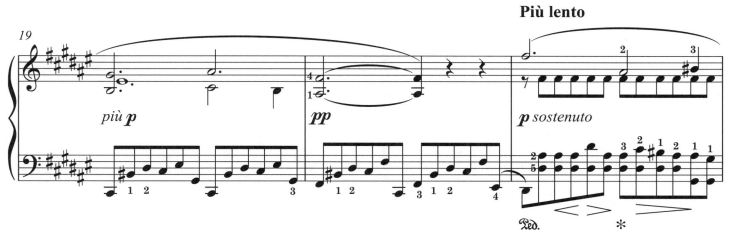

Più lento

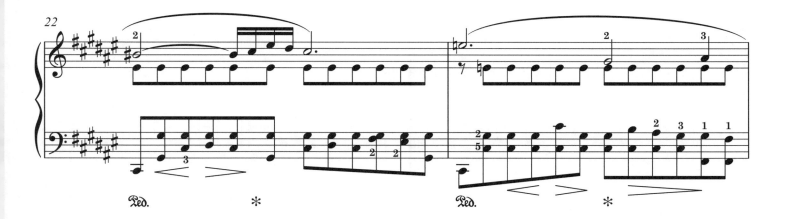

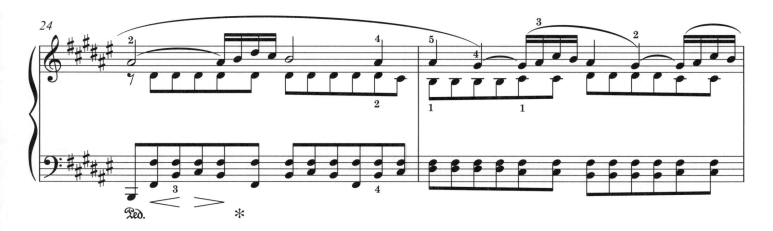

84

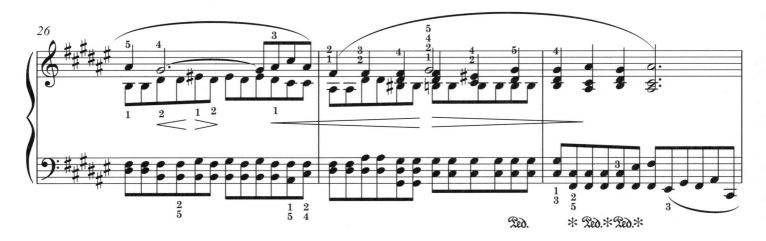

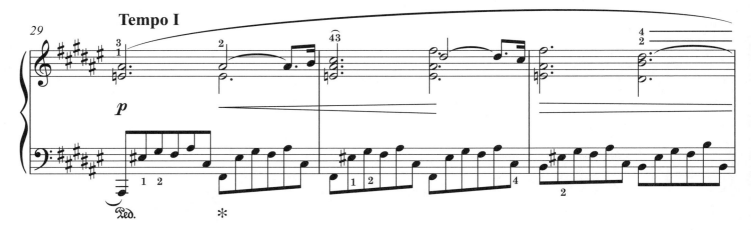

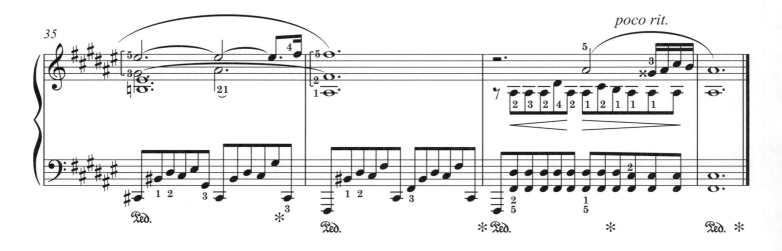

I Call to You, Lord Jesus Christ

Ich ruf zu Dir, Herr

Johann Sebastian Bach
1685–1750
Arr.: Ferruccio Busoni

Andante (♪ = 50)
Mit Andacht
Die Oberstimme sehr ausdrucksvoll und gehalten
Molto espressivo e tenuto il canto

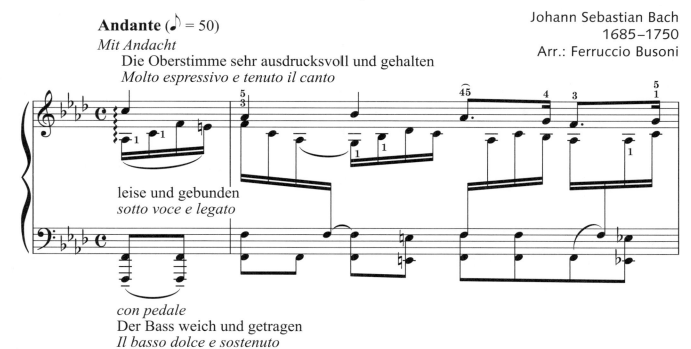

leise und gebunden
sotto voce e legato

con pedale
Der Bass weich und getragen
Il basso dolce e sostenuto

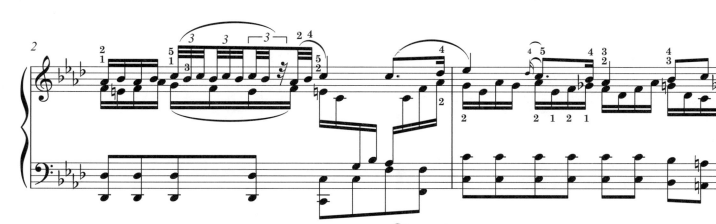

poco slentando

più dolce

sehr weich

From the Schott edition *Concert Favourites* (ED 21827)

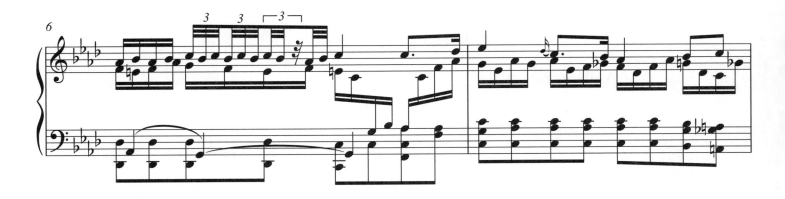

etwas heller
poco più sonore

più **p**

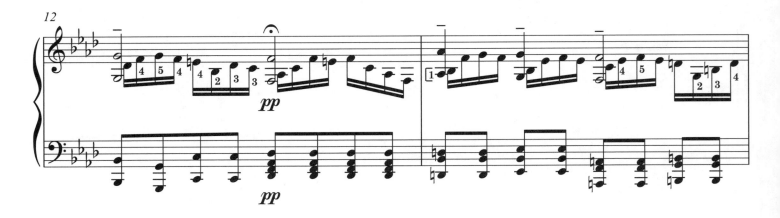

pp

pp

poco aumentando

calando _ _ _ _ _ _ _ _ _

ten.

poco

più oscuro, ma sempre cantando

molto legato

pp

Elegy

from *Morceaux de fantaisie*, Op. 3/1

Sergei Rachmaninoff
1873–1943

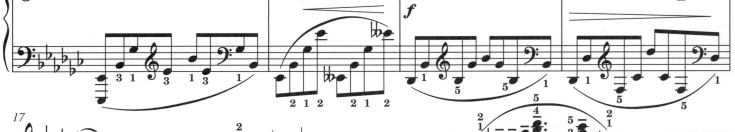

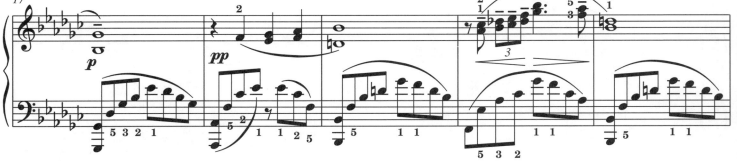

From the Schott edition *Emotions* (ED 9045)

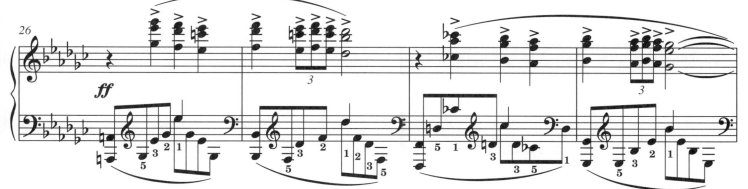

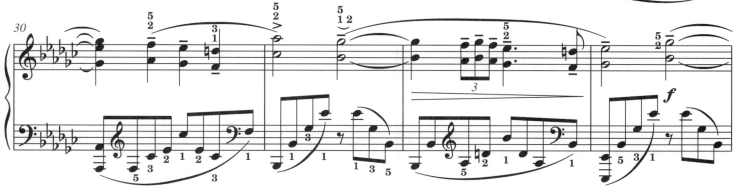

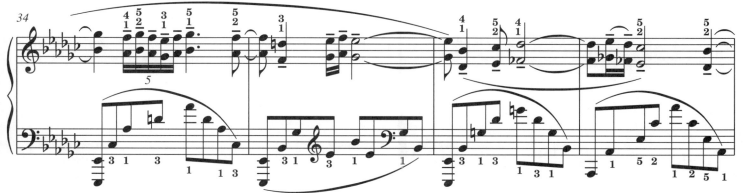

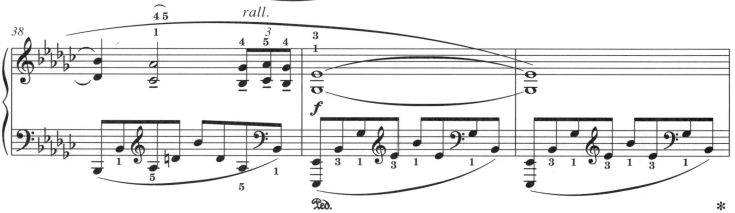

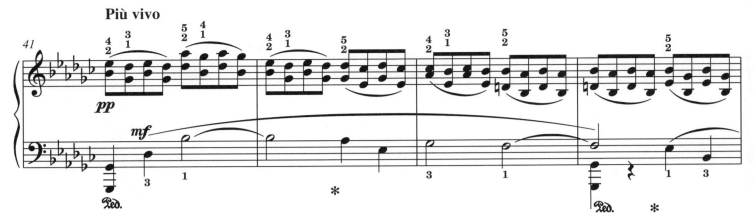

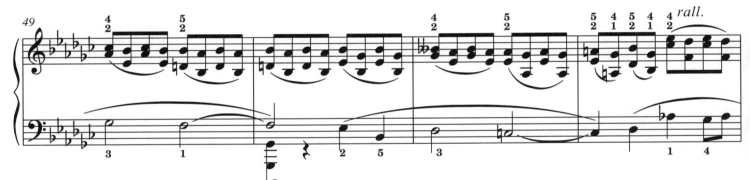

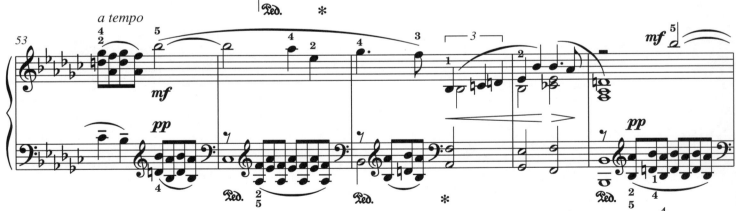

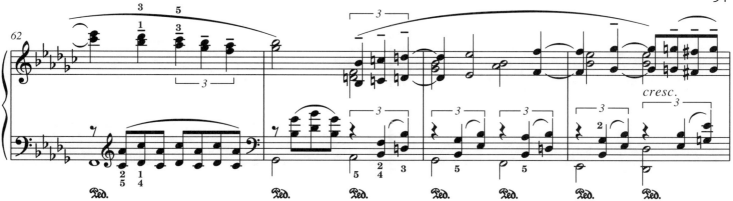

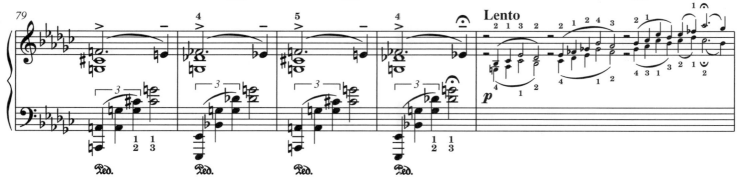

Tempo I

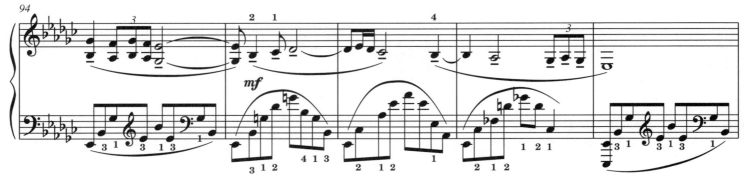